Text © Sydney Wood, 1981
Illustrations © Macmillan Publishers Limited 1981

First published in 1981 by
Macmillan Children's Books
a division of Macmillan Publishers Limited
4 Little Essex Street, London WC2R 3LF
and Basingstoke
Associated companies thoughout the world.

Printed in Hong Kong

ISBN 0 333 31307 0

Editor: Miranda Ferguson
Designer: Julian Holland
Adviser: Patrick Whitehouse
Picture Researchers: John and Diane Moore
                        Stella Martin
Photo credits:
AMTRAK; Association of American Railroads, USA;
Austrian State Railways; Baltimore and Ohio Railroad Museum;
BBC Hulton Picture Library; British Railway Board;
Colourviews Picture Library; G. P. Cooper; Cooper-Bridgeman;
D. Cross; Deutsches Bundesbahn, Mainz; EMI Films;
Mary Evans Picture Library; Fujifotos, Tokyo; C. J. Gammell;
J. Holland; Italian State Railways, Rome; London Transport;
Mansell Collection; MARS; Museum of British Transport;
National Railway Museum, York; New Zealand Railways;
Ivo Peters; Railways of Australia; RATP; G. R. Roberts;
Santa Fe Railway; Science Museum; SNCF; B. Stephenson;
Tweetsie Railroad; Union Pacific Railroad Museum Collection,
Nebraska; Victoria and Albert Museum; Peter Newark's
Western Americana; C. M. Whitehouse; P. B. Whitehouse;
Wuppertaler Stadtwerke AG; ZEFA

Wood, Sydney
 The railway revolution.
 1. Railroads – Juvenile literature
 I. Title
 385   HG1037

 ISBN 0-333-31307-0

The Railway Revolution

Sydney Wood

M

Contents

Rice paddy-fields in Sumatra reflect the image of a train, which is busily working its way across the countryside. The railways opened up the Far East, and facilitated trading.

Introduction

Railways have fascinated people for over 150 years. The many hundreds of books written about railways include not only histories and scientific descriptions, but also tales of mystery and adventure in which trains play a key role. Pictures of trains, past and present, can be found on the postage stamps of many countries. The railway past is preserved in museums and in old railway lines lovingly restored by volunteers.

Why do railways have such a magical appeal? This book explores in words and pictures some of the reasons why railways have been, and remain, so deeply interesting to so many people. From their beginnings in Britain, it was clear that railways were going to play a most important part in changing the lives of people around the world.

Building and running the railways provided work for thousands of people, made some men's fortunes and ruined others. Huge problems had to be overcome as railway track snaked across deserts, passed through mountains and spanned great rivers. Special types of railway were invented that could clamber to the very peaks of mountains or burrow deep beneath city streets.

Through the power of machines, railways totally transformed human travel, opening up parts of the world to people who had been no further than their home towns before. The great steam locomotives, breathing fire and smoke, were foremost in this, and names like the *Orient Express* became legendary. For a time, the huge network of world railways seemed in danger of shrinking away before the menace of new machines. But today, the challenge of cars, lorries and aircraft has been met by the development of new types of track and train. Railways are too important to be allowed to disappear.

The might and majesty of steam power can be seen in this locomotive of the French Railways (SNCF) on the line near Abbeville, just after a thunderstorm.

Beginnings

Before Railways

For many centuries the moving of heavy goods has been a key factor in people's attempts to improve their lives. Farmers need to send away the produce of their land and bring in fertilizers and foodstuffs for animals. Manufacturers need machines and have to transport the things that they make. Ordinary people need bricks, slates and timber for housebuilding, and all sorts of other items for fuel, food and clothing.

Before railways developed, water transport provided by far the best and cheapest method of shifting bulky goods. Towns prospered that were close by ports or near to rivers along which vessels could safely sail. In pre-railway Britain alone, there were 1,000 miles of navigable rivers.

The Old East India Quay in London (right) was always full of bustling activity. Merchantmen like these sailing vessels not only ventured to other lands, but supplied an essential link between places on the coast of the same country. A long sea-journey in the pre-railway age provided cheaper transport than a short overland route could offer.

A scene on the Paddington Canal (below) in 1840. There was a great growth in canal-building in late 18th-century Britain. A horse, pulling a barge, could manage to haul a 50-ton load. But barges moved very slowly, canals froze in winter, and for people living in hilly areas canals were no help.

Early Transport

'I walked several miles on foot, met 20 wagons tearing their goods to pieces and the drivers cursing,' wrote a British traveller in 1752. Overland travel by coach and waggon was indeed difficult in the pre-railway age, and likely to be at no more than walking-speed. Pack ponies moved easily but could manage no more than 240-pound loads apiece. So the introduction of ruts or rails to move waggons was welcomed by all those seeking to shift heavy loads.

Ancient Greek and Roman civilizations have both left examples of stone rutways down which rolled trucks carrying stone slabs. Wooden rails were certainly being laid in Germany by the 16th century. German miners used them and so did pitmen in northern England. During the later 18th century iron rails were beginning to replace the wooden ones. Some of these 'plateways' had flanges (rims) to keep the waggons on the rails, while others used flanged wheels and flat rails.

Changing Horses at the Relay House ·1830·

Oxen were often used to pull trucks, and can sometimes be seen still, like these oxen with the produce of a sugar-cane harvest (above). It was in areas where bulky goods had to be shifted that railways began, and they are still used in the transport of goods.

The construction of the Baltimore-Ohio Line in the USA began in 1828, and by 1830, 14 miles of double-track were being worked by horses. In this picture (left), they are changing horses at the relay house during horse-drawn operations.

The horses drawing waggons along the line (right) are working a route that first opened in 1793 and connected Belvoir Castle with the Grantham Canal. Horses were probably the most common form of haulage power on these routes. Where track ran downhill, the horses were often provided with 'dandy' carts in which they could ride. The East Midlands were a pioneering area in tramway development. In 1605, Sir Francis Willoughby had created a two-mile track from his Wollaton coal-mine down to the River Trent.

Steam Power

Though the power of steam had been recognized for 2,000 years, it was not until the early 18th century that it was harnessed for serious practical work. In 1712, a Devonshire blacksmith, Thomas Newcomen, created an 'atmospheric' engine that successfully pumped flood-water from the tin-mines of Cornwall. The Newcomen engines were slow, heavy and ate up huge amounts of fuel. Their power came from the rapid cooling of steam fed in below the piston so that a vacuum was created and the piston sank down.

These pumping engines were made much more powerful and efficient by James Watt (in 1777 he devised a separate condenser to cool the steam) but they remained so vast that it was unthinkable that they could ever power locomotives. Watt later adapted them to turn machinery round and round, not just up and down. But towards inventors who worked on manufacturing steam carriages, Watt remained resolutely hostile.

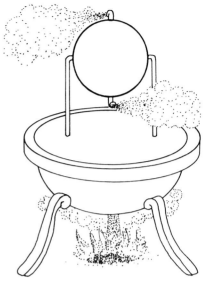

This strange device (above) was a steam-filled ball that whirled round as the steam escaped from its opposing jets. Its creator was Hero, a Greek inhabitant of Alexandria nearly 2,000 years ago.

The 1827 steam-car owner (below) is pleading: 'My friend, give my car some coke; your coal is too expensive.'

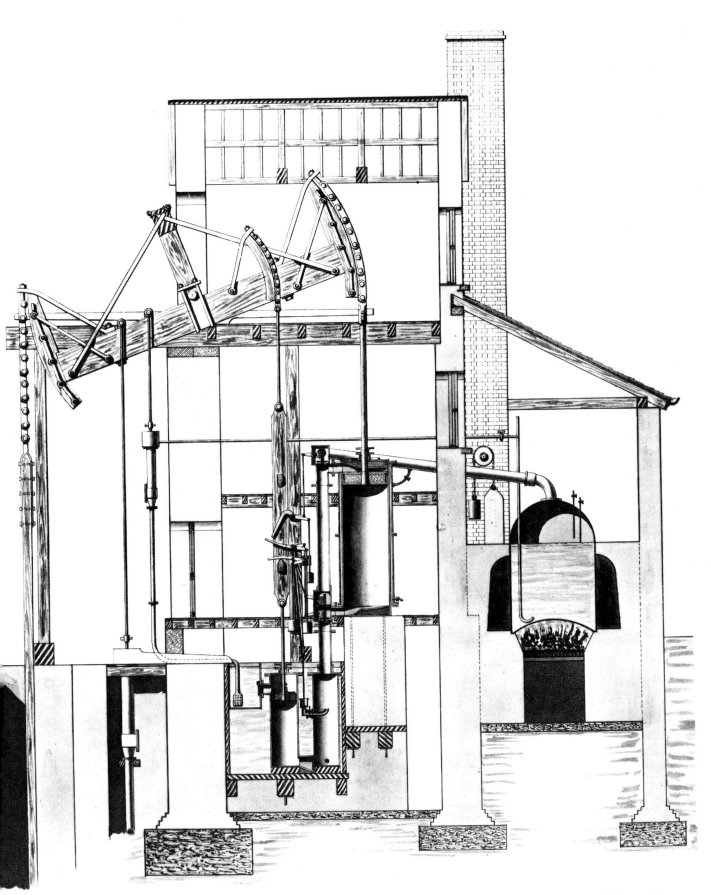

This steam-pumping engine was designed in 1788 by the great Scottish inventor, James Watt (1736-1819). It is a single-beam engine intended for the draining of mines. Machines like this did much to improve the safety of the men working in the coal-mines.

In order to make a steam engine that could drive a wheeled vehicle, it was necessary to produce a design that was compact and powerful. This meant building up a high pressure of steam and James Watt, who was a very cautious man, thought this was much too risky.

Yet by the time Watt began to work on this problem, a Frenchman, Denis Papin, had already designed a safety valve that greatly reduced the danger of disaster. Papin wanted to make a high-pressure steam container so that he could cook juice out of bones.

Papin's fellow Frenchman, Nicholas Cugnot, had more practical plans. In 1769, Cugnot astonished crowds in Paris by driving through the streets in a strange three-wheeled steam-powered machine. It reached a speed of nine miles an hour and then turned over and blew up. The authorities seized the object, and clapped Cugnot in prison.

A very lively scene in Regent's Park, London (left). The artist who produced this drawing in 1831 was very impressed by the coming of steam power and dreamed of all sorts of machines that would soon be trundling around in Britain's streets. He was obviously a bit carried away by his imagination. Not all of his designs look entirely safe!

One of the most active experimenters with early steam carriages in Britain was James Watt's own foreman, William Murdoch. Murdoch produced a model steam carriage that ran along the lanes around Redruth after dark. The local vicar is said to have been terrified by a glimpse of this smoke-belching beast. Watt frowned on this work and it was left to an enterprising Cornishman, Richard Trevithick, to pursue it more vigorously. Trevithick, Watt declared, deserved to be hanged for building such risky machines.

A number of inventors produced steam carriages that ran along quite successfully. This machine is an 1832 design by Macerone and Squire. The man on the right is feeding the carriage with coal. The weight of steam engines was always a problem. Early locomotives, put on wooden track, often smashed up the rails as they ran along.

The First Engineers

In the early 19th century, several men struggled to develop successful steam locomotives. In 1804, Richard Trevithick constructed an engine that was impressively powerful. However, the smooth rails it ran on seemed too slippery to other engineers. When Matthew Murray built a locomotive for John Blenkinsop, the latter insisted that its driving wheels be fitted with a cog that slotted into toothed track.

In 1813, William Hedley proved that his *Puffing Billy* could steam successfully along smooth track to Wylam Colliery, Newcastle. Hedley's near neighbour, George Stephenson, was just beginning to apply his great skill to building improved locomotives.

George Stephenson and his son Robert were to contribute a great deal to the development of the railways.

Running round this track (below) is the locomotive, *Catch Me Who Can*. It was designed by a remarkable Cornish tin-mining engineer, Richard Trevithick. His first locomotive won a bet in 1804 by pulling a ten-ton load of iron down a ten-mile track. In 1808, for a shilling, people could enter this circular enclosure in London's suburbs at Euston, to watch *Catch Me Who Can*. The inventor was always short of money, and an accident he could not afford to repair ended the entertainment. He tried vainly to make his fortune in South America before returning home to die, poor and forgotten.

The Stephenson family (above) were the children of Robert, a Northumberland fireman whose home was a small cottage. The sons worked at developing railways but George's self-taught practical skills made him the most famous. Helped by other engineers, he built a series of engines for the north-east coalfields.

Locomotion (right), ran from Stockton to Darlington in 1825, pulling coal waggons and one passenger coach.

15

The Rainhill Trials

On 6th October 1829, great crowds gathered round a short stretch of railway track near Liverpool. They had come to marvel at the mysteries of steam locomotion and to guess which of several competitors would win a prize offered by the directors of the new Manchester-Liverpool line.

It was planned to show haulage by stationary steam engines, but first, locomotive engineers competed for the chance to supply engines. Locomotives should not weigh over six tons (the track could not take massive weights) and they were to run up and down a 1½-mile length of track until they had travelled the same distance as a return trip between Manchester and Liverpool.

A horse-powered entry and the locomotive *Perseverance* could not manage the required average speed of ten miles an hour. The crowds were very taken with the *Novelty*, which whizzed up and down at over 30 miles an hour, but it broke down far too frequently. Since the *Sans Pareil* broke down too, it was left to the Stephensons' *Rocket* to prove to doubters that steam engines were reliable enough to work the railways.

The *Rocket* covered 70 miles without fault at an average speed of 15 miles an hour, though George and Robert also took her up to 29 miles an hour. On 15th October, George Stephenson proudly stepped up to receive £500, having completely convinced the directors that *Rocket*-type locomotives could safely work their new line.

In J. Wooton's painting (above right), three of the Rainhill competitors are getting ready to take it in turn to run up and down the track. *Novelty, Rocket* and *Sans Pareil* were the three most famous locomotives to take part in the trials. *Novelty* was built by John Braithwaite and John Ericsson. It was a fast engine, but the bellows were unreliable.

Rocket carried her water in a barrel. Her boiler-water was heated by 25 copper tubes instead of a single flue, which greatly improved her steaming power. *Sans Pareil* was built by the Stephensons' colleague, Timothy Hackworth. He had to work hastily. His engine suffered several breakdowns and gobbled up huge quantities of fuel.

The Novelty

The Rocket

The Sans Pareil

The First Modern Railway

On the morning of 15th September 1830, the crash of cannon-shot marked the opening of the first modern public railway to provide steam-hauled trains for the people.

George Stephenson engineered the route. His biggest problem had been laying track across the bleak waste of Chat Moss, in which stones sank. It was only by pouring in endless piles of brushwood and heather that a sufficiently solid base was built up.

To open the line, Stephenson himself drove the *Northumbrian* from Liverpool to Manchester – with the Prime Minister, the Duke of Wellington, as passenger. Huge crowds gathered and a band played in a carriage attached to the Duke's coach.

At Parkside, where the engines stopped to take on water, the Liverpool M.P. William Huskisson left the train. As the *Rocket* came up another track, Huskisson panicked, fell in its path and died from his injuries. Despite this, the line made over £14,000 profit in three months and put half the stagecoaches on the route out of business.

The line carried both goods and passengers (above). Here, two 1833 trains are carrying a variety of traffic including live animals.

Parkside Station, 1830 (below) with an engine taking on water for the boiler. The station had no platform.

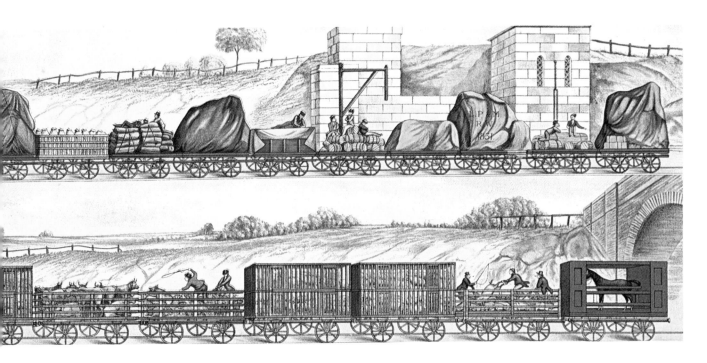

The line involved engineering works that, at the time, seemed quite an achievement.
The 'Moorish Arch' (left) at Liverpool, was the line's main ornamental work and concealed a stationary steam engine. It was not George Stephenson's design and was later taken down. Stephenson's Bridge at Rainhill below was one of 63 bridges that he built. He also had to plan a viaduct over the Sankey Canal, a tunnel and the deep Olive Mount cutting.

Isambard Kingdom Brunel

Between 1830 and 1860 a massive railway network was developed in Britain. This growth provided great opportunities for men able to plan and build new lines, and of these none was more impressive than Isambard Kingdom Brunel.

Brunel was born in 1806, and his education was carefully planned by his engineer father, first at school in England and then in French academies where sciences were well taught. He possessed great energy, imagination and practical skills, and designed works as varied as railways, bridges, stations and docks. When a coin he had swallowed stuck in his throat, he even designed a gadget to help baffled surgeons remove it. He died aged 53, leaving memorials like the Saltash Bridge shown here (far right).

Confusion reigns at Gloucester station (above) where passengers and their luggage had to change trains between standard and broad-gauge services. When a Parliamentary Commission investigating gauge sizes visited the station, the standard-gauge companies organized as much confusion as possible.

One of Brunel's masterpieces was the Saltash Bridge over the Cornish River Tamar (above right). It was opened in 1859 by Prince Albert, a few months before Brunel's death. Two huge spans of 455 feet rested on a central pier.

The engine-house at the Great Western Railway works at Swindon (left), and (inset) a portrait of Brunel. In the centre of the picture is one of the 2-2-2 engines designed by the Locomotive Superintendent, Daniel Gooch. A whole new town developed around the works.

In 1833 Brunel was appointed engineer to a new line planned to link London to Bristol. To create this Great Western Railway, he had to survey the route, persuade Parliament of its merits, employ a huge workforce, and design and supervise the building of bridges, tunnels and stations. Anxious landlords had to be calmed, and angry landlords avoided by a re-routing of the line.

Brunel's plans were always ambitious and, at the time, many people declared that the bridge he designed to take track over the Thames would collapse. They also said that his 3,000-yard Box Hill tunnel was unsafe. A huge two-mile cutting at Sonning proved too difficult for two other contractors, so Brunel supervised the 1,220 workmen himself. He also designed the railway track, laying it along great timbers, with a width of 7 feet between the rails. Most of Britain followed the 4 foot 8½ inch gauge that Stephenson had copied from north-eastern waggonways, but Brunel insisted that his trains would run more safely and speedily.

In 1844, the first train steamed from London to Brunel's magnificent new station at Temple Meads, Bristol. Not until 1892 was the broad gauge finally scrapped on the Great Western Railway.

Enemies of Development

All sorts of people were very suspicious of the arrival of the railway. Some were most concerned about the danger of travelling on trains, while others thought that railways would wreck the countryside and ruin the productivity of farm animals. Brunel had to shift the Great Western Railway three miles away from Eton to avoid the anger of an important headmaster who feared his pupils would be distracted. On the other hand, the Duke of Wellington believed railways would quite alter British society by enabling ordinary people to travel.

The colourful poster of 1876 (below) is advertising the stagecoach services of the New York company of J.B. Brewster. Stagecoaches found it especially hard to compete with the speed, comfort and low fares of the railways. It is not surprising that they were against the introduction of steam trains for the trains ruined their passenger and mail services and damaged the trade at many of the inns along the roadside. Turnpike roads in Britain fell into a sad state of decay in the mid-19th century.

The hunt is pursuing the fox even though this means crossing the railway-line (left). It has been said that several British lines were delayed while land-owners were persuaded that railways would not ruin the hunting.

A *Punch* cartoon of 1846 (below) shows a steam locomotive being arrested. The 'policeman' is in fact a politician of the times called Sibthorpe, who was famous for being against the changes brought about by the railways.

A DANGEROUS CHARACTER.

Laying the Tracks
Railroads Come to North America

In the early 19th century, most of the USA's eight million people lived in widely scattered settlements along the coastal belts, divided by rivers and with mountains, prairies or deserts further inland. Early American settlers, seeking to improve transport, concentrated on making roads or canals; early American steam enthusiasts usually put their engines in the many boats that travelled the rivers, lakes and canals.

When, in 1813, Oliver Evans suggested a railway from New York to Philadelphia, no one took him seriously. He had to make do with building a steam carriage.

In 1830 the owners of the recently opened Baltimore and Ohio Line allowed a wealthy glue-maker, Peter Cooper, to race his tiny locomotive *Tom Thumb* against one of their horse-drawn trains. *Tom Thumb*'s vertical boiler was filled with flues made from sawn-off musket barrels. Cooper's engine was unluckily beaten in the race when a belt-drive in its workings slipped. However, steam engines gradually took over on the route.

Steam locomotives began to work the Baltimore-Ohio's 14 miles in 1830. Here, the *Atlantic* is hauling a train.

The opening of the first Canadian Railway on 21st July 1836 (right). The line ran from Laprairie to St Johns, linking the St Lawrence River to the Lake Champlain River system.

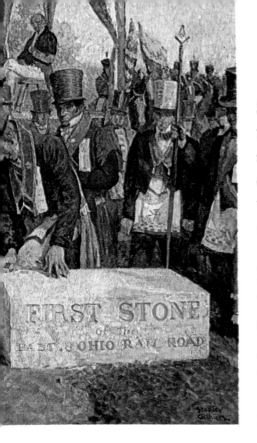

In 1828, the first stone in the building of the Baltimore-Ohio line, USA, was laid (above). The army surveyed the route, the main feature of which was a viaduct named after Charles Caroll, who laid the stone.

In 1829, Horatio Allen became Chief Engineer to the new South Carolina Railroad linking Charleston on the coast to the riverside town of Hamburg, opposite the expanding settlement of Augusta. Allen was just recovering from the disappointing rejection of the *Stourbridge Lion* by the Delaware and Hudson Company. The company feared that his engine was too heavy for the trestle bridge on the line.

For his new line, Allen ordered four engines to be built locally at the West Point Foundry. On 2nd November 1830, the first *Best Friend of Charleston* steamed successfully along and was soon managing speeds of 20 miles an hour. On 15th January 1831, the USA's first public-service steam railroad opened for business, hauling a train that contained not only a brass band, but also a party of soldiers with a light field-gun firing blanks.

By 1833, the line's six miles had extended to 135 miles, though by then the accident-prone *Best Friend* was out of action. In June 1831, her fireman, a Negro boy, annoyed by the loud hissing of the safety valve, tied it down. Unfortunately the boiler blew up, the fireman died from his injuries and the driver was badly scalded.

Spanning the USA

In 1856, the Rock Island Line built a huge 1,583-foot bridge over that mighty obstacle to railway expansion to the west – the Mississippi River. The population of the USA was growing (in the 1840s 4½ million people poured in from Europe) and land-hungry farmers were pushing westwards.

Railway growth meant that great inland communities which relied on farming could expand, like Chicago where 11 railway lines met. There, local hoteliers provided roof-top telescopes so that businessmen could watch for the arrival of the all-important train.

Track-laying is in progress in 1880 on the Northern Pacific's line through western North Dakota (right). Once the line was surveyed, 'graders' moved in to cut, fill and bridge-build. Close behind followed an army of track-layers spiking down the rails.

Moving west in the pre-railway age was a slow and dangerous business. These travellers in 1866 (below) are passing under the shadow of the mighty Rocky Mountains. They have provisions for several months.

On 2nd December 1863, railroad workers (including 15 Indian squaws) began work on the Union Pacific Railroad's greatest enterprise. A line was planned which would stretch westwards across the USA from Omaha, Nebraska. Snaking eastwards to meet it came the track of the Central Pacific line. The project was helped by loans and generous land grants by a government which was eager to see the USA linked together by railway lines.

Cheyenne Indians, led by Tall Bull, are tearing up the track of the hated Iron Horse that had invaded their lands at Fossil Creek, Kansas in 1869. The seven trackmen they surprised fled on a handcar; two were killed and four wounded.

For six years the railroad builders of the two companies battled to build track and, at times, held off attacks from Indians who were horrified by this invasion of their lands. The Union Pacific's labour force included many Irishmen, and the Central Pacific employed 6,000 Chinese for the treacherous task of blasting through the rocks of the Sierra Nevada mountains.

As the track grew, so did settlements along its line. Some, designed to serve the railroad men, came to be known as 'Hell on Wheels', so grim was life in them and so easily were they pulled down and rebuilt elsewhere. The railroad companies made great profits from the miles of track that they laid; they were even beginning to build parallel to one another when the Government made them link up.

The meeting of the Central Pacific's *Jupiter* and No.119 of the Union Pacific took place on 10th May 1869, at Promontory Point, Utah (above). They tapped in golden spikes.

The railways played a vital part in the growth and prosperity of countless towns across the USA (right). It also enabled many people to travel vast distances in comfort.

28

The Railway Kings

In Britain, the growth of railways helped some men, who were skilful at organizing, to make a lot of money. At first there were not many rules to control what people planning and running railway lines were allowed to do, and some of them made fortunes by very ruthless activities. George Hudson was the most famous of these 'Railway Kings' in Britain.

These men were good at managing companies, persuading people to put their money into railways and capturing control of lines that might help or rival their own. But it was in the USA, from the 1860s to the 1880s, that the really remarkable 'Railway Kings' were busy battling with each other. They were unscrupulous men, whose aim was to make a fortune, not serve travellers. The line that first crossed the USA was soon found to be full of shoddy, and even dangerous workmanship. In Georgia, Hannibal Kimball even managed to make a fortune from state help for railway building, without laying any track at all! Elsewhere travellers were heavily overcharged.

In this cartoon (right) Commodore Vanderbilt is trying to capture the Erie Railroad from Jay Gould, one of the great 'Robber Barons' of American railway history. Gould was a skilful and ruthless man. His control over the Erie Line, won in 1869, was but one of many successes. In 25 years he increased his million-dollar fortune 80-fold, and on the way ruined many men. So much money was squeezed from his lines that they were left in a poor condition.

The Hudson Testimonial.

This cartoon of 1846 (left) shows what could be built to mark the career of a former York linen draper, George Hudson. From the lines he captured and created, Hudson built up the large Midland Company. He knew nothing of actual practical railway working, but his skill with money seemed to make him very rich and powerful. Several of his schemes failed, however, and he was disgraced and ruined, living his last years on money provided by friends.

THE GREAT RACE FOR THE WESTERN STAKES 1870

Cornelius Vanderbilt, grandson of the Commodore, ran the family business very skilfully for many years.

Oakes Ames made a fortune by selling shovels to the Union Pacific, and then rose to head the company.

Thomas Scott was important in several railway projects. He battled for the power and profits the railways provided.

The European Network

In the early 19th century, the countries of Continental Europe needed railways even more than Britain if they were going to grow richer and more powerful. Much of inland Europe was remote from any reliable system of transport. Yet many European countries had too few men of wealth and skill to leave the development of railways to the sort of individual effort that had worked so well in Britain.

From the start, many European kings and princes followed the example of Leopold of Belgium. Between 1835 and 1844, Belgium obtained a largely British-built and government-organized railway system.

Some rulers, like the kings of Naples and Spain, feared the railways. They believed that the changes the railways brought about would upset their countries so much that royal power would be weakened. However, other rulers welcomed the trains. Not only did they carry goods and people, they also shifted soldiers easily to trouble spots and thus increased government power.

In the mid-19th century, Italy was not a single state with one government. It was split up into separate areas, each with their own rulers. In the north lay the Kingdom of Piedmont, ruled by Victor Emmanuel II. His very skilful chief minister, Count Cavour, wanted to see Piedmont lead the joining together of the different states.

Cavour believed that railway-building would make his country stronger. In 1854, the King opened a new railway link which joined the important cities of Genoa and Turin.

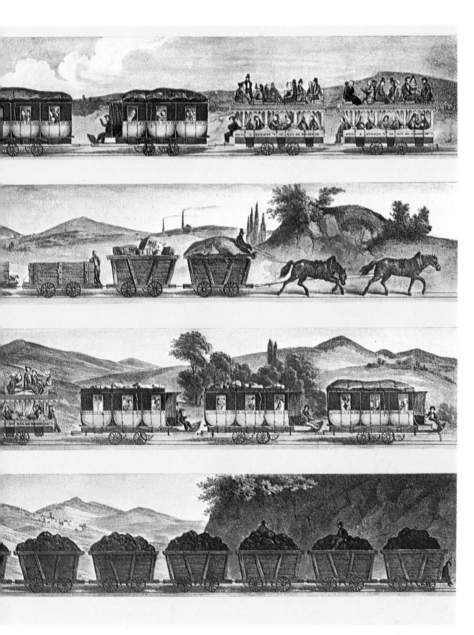

In 1829, various kinds of traffic could be seen running along a 38-mile line from St Etienne to Lyons in France (left). The line had opened in 1828, and was originally worked by horses, but soon it was being operated by two steam locomotives designed by Marc Seguin, which were very similar to the Stephensons' *Rocket.* It was the local coal-mines that attracted railway-builders to St Etienne, but passengers too were carried on the line, some of them in doubledecker coaches.

Like Italy, mid-19th century Germany was not a single state. Several German princes encouraged railway-building, and so many of them used the Stephenson gauge of track that it was not very difficult to join together separate systems. The illustrations (below) show early railway scenes in Saxony, including the station at Leipzig from which, in 1839, trains ran to Dresden. The line was opened by a German-built locomotive, *Saxonia.*

Russia and the Trans-Siberian

The vast, sprawling mass of 19th-century Russia seemed to its rulers, the Czars, to need railways for two main reasons. Firstly, the power of the Czars would be much strengthened if they were able to speedily move troops to put down rebellions or beat back enemies. Secondly, the wealth of Russia would be greatly increased if railways could open up new farmland and new sources of coal and iron.

The Russian government had to find the money for schemes which reached a peak in 1891 with plans that spanned the whole country. So bleak were parts of Russia that great armies of convicts, watched closely by troops, had to be used to complete a line across Russia that finally opened in 1905. The line promptly proved its value: grain production rose and Siberia's population swelled.

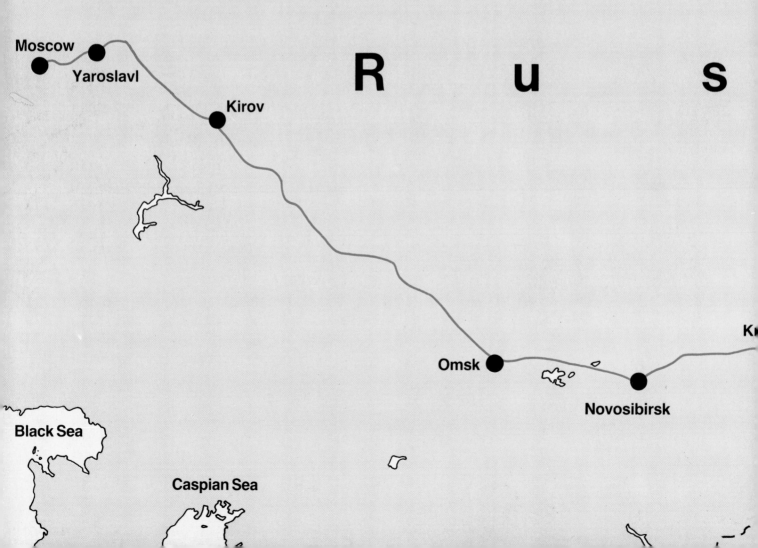

A train is taking soldiers (left) to fight in a Far-Eastern war against Japan that raged from 1904-5. Children (right) sold flowers at stations on the Trans-Siberian route.

The huge extent of Russia is spanned by a line linking Europe to the far reaches of Asia. At first, the eastern section ran through China. The modern section shown here (below), the 'Amur Loop', was built from 1908 to 1916. The Lake Beikal section was worked at first by ferries.

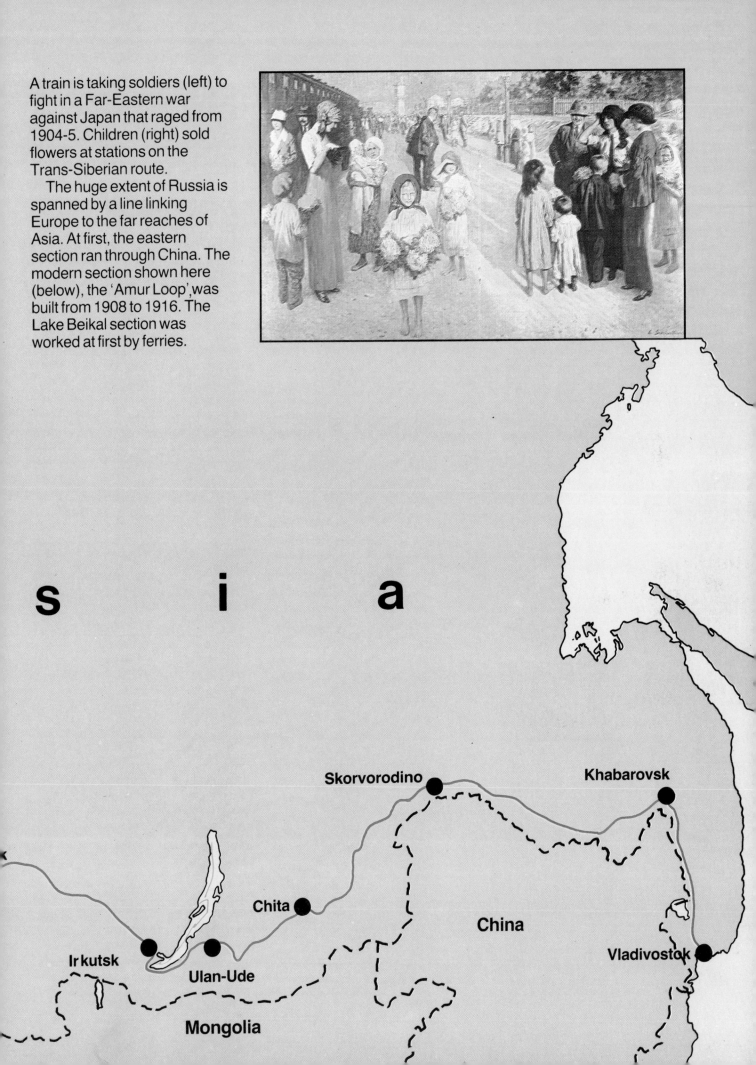

s i a

Skorvorodino

Khabarovsk

Chita

China

Irkutsk

Ulan-Ude

Vladivostok

Mongolia

Australia and New Zealand

The country of Australia stretches over nearly three million square miles. Though its population grew in the 19th century, it was still small and widely scattered in a series of separate colonies around the coast. Railways first developed not so much to link up important places, as to open up the interior and help Australians develop farming and mining industries.

A train steams along beside water in New Zealand (above). Railways provide remote places in the interior with a link to the coast.

Horse-drawn lines and even a five-mile track in Tasmania worked by convicts pushing trucks, were gradually replaced by steam power. In New Zealand, too, short stretches of track probed into the interior, linking it to the coast. But whereas New Zealand used a 3 foot 6 inch track, in Australia many different gauge lines were built.

In 1901, the six separate Australian colonies became one country. It is hard to see how this could have been done without the spread of the railway. The building of a line 1,051 miles long right across the country, between 1911 and 1917, was a further sign of railroad progress.

This early picture (below) shows a train system of the Australian Railways and the buildings that sprang up around it.

South America

The railway systems that developed in South America in the late 19th century depended very heavily on foreign money, skill and materials. Only the labour was local, and many hundreds of labourers gave their lives in the building of lines through the dangerous mountain regions of the Andes. The magnet that attracted foreigners, especially British and American engineers and financiers, was the money to be made in farming and finding minerals.

Railway-builders in Peru faced huge problems. This train, on Peru's National Railway line, is passing through a canyon near Machu Picchu. The mountain scenery may be picturesque, but it was very difficult to tame with track. However, the effort seems to have been worthwhile, because the more barren coastline is now linked to the richer farming valleys, and to areas where nitrates, copper and silver are found.

Africa

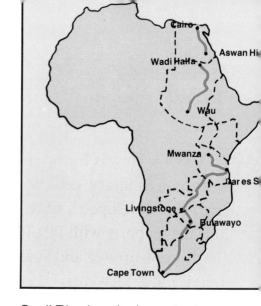

Several European states won control of most of the African continent in the late 19th century. With them, they brought the skills and materials needed to construct railways. A line from Alexandria to Cairo engineered by Robert Stephenson and opened in 1856, started this development.

In east Africa, British possessions were so extensive that they were able to plan to link up the lines in different colonies. Elsewhere, there were railways built by the French, Belgians, Germans and Italians.

Today, Europe's control over Africa has gone, but the new governments continue to recognize the importance of railways. They help to make the individual countries richer, and also join up different tribes to form nations.

Cecil Rhodes, the important British leader in South Africa in the late 19th century began the work on the Cape to Cairo Railway, but it was never quite finished (above).

Steam power flourished in Africa, as here (below) on this Ugandan line to Kampala.

The Orient

In Asia, too, it was European skill and money that followed European military conquest and built railways. British engineers developed a system in India that was designed to link the seaports with inland centres. Cities and industrial towns grew up, tea and sugar growing increased, and coal and cotton cloth were produced in far bigger quantities once railways arrived in the Far East.

The first line, from Bombay in 1853, was rapidly followed by more track aimed at helping the British rulers control the country, as well as at increasing its wealth. Today, the railway systems, although they are not the most modern in the world, still provide links to many parts of the Far East which otherwise would be entirely cut off.

A Baldwin-built 0-6-0 is being serviced on a sugar plantation in Java in 1975. The railway systems in the Far East have given a vital life-line to people who need to transport their crops, medicines, clothes and food. Many of the trains, however, are very old and they frequently break down.

Locomotives
Evolution of the Steam Locomotive

The evolution of the steam locomotive was gradual, and these are just a few of the major structural types and their special features.

1838   In the 1830s and 1840s, Edward Bury built engines like this for the London and Birmingham Railway. His partner was James Kennedy. Bury had meant to enter an engine for the Rainhill trials, but he was too late. American engineers copied the bar-frame from his designs.

1845   The tall smoke-stack of this early American engine was designed as a 'spark arrester' to stop damage resulting from flying fragments of fire. Edward Bury developed this design in an attempt to burn hard coal, not coke. American locomotives used the device in order to burn wood safely.

1849   A French example of a long-boilered type of engine developed in the 1840s by Robert Stephenson. The boiler design was meant to produce a better use of fuel, but it made the early models unstable, and several fell off the rails at speed. This design had an extra pair of trailing wheels.

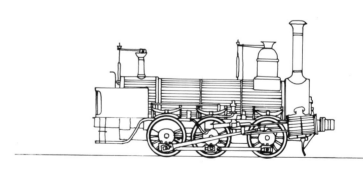

1857   An American engineer, Thomas Rogers, lengthened the wheelbase of the front bogie and brought the cylinders to a level position. This design by Danforth Cooke follows Rogers' pattern. This engine features a cowcatcher. Collisions with cows derailed several locomotives.

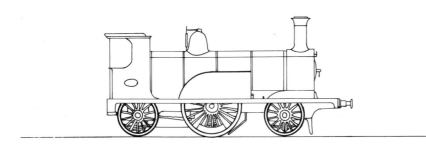

1881 A locomotive designed by William Stroudley for the London, Brighton and South Coast Railway. By this time, improved iron and steel meant that a neater design could be produced. Just two wheels drove the engine. When trains became very heavy this made them slip when starting.

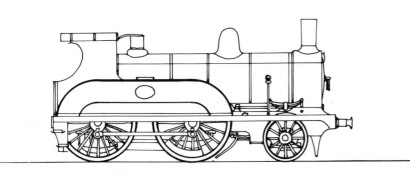

1882 On this locomotive (designed by T. W. Worsdell for Great Eastern Railways) the driving wheels were coupled, and they were seven feet in diameter. Engines like this were used to pull many of Britain's passenger expresses towards the end of the 19th century.

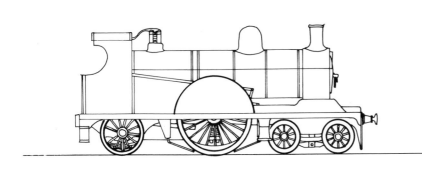

1889 One of the later locomotives with a single pair of driving wheels. Its four-wheel front bogie helped it ride well at high speeds, while the problem of slipping when starting was partially solved by a steam-sounding invention. This engine was designed by H. Pollitt for the Great Central.

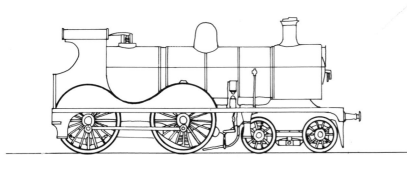

1908 This type of express locomotive was to be found on every major British railway of the early 20th century. The leading bogie helped carry the weight of the engine, and assisted fast, smooth running. The cylinders were not to be seen, being tucked away inside the frame.

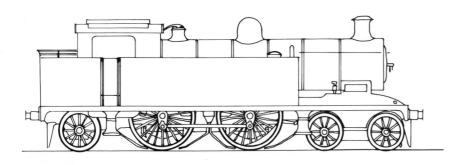

1910 D.E. Marsh designed locomotives like this to haul fast trains on the London-Brighton service. It was a tank engine carrying fuel in its main frame, not in a separate tender. In 1910, one of these machines was fitted with a superheater designed by Dr Wilhelm Schmidt.

How a Steam Locomotive Works

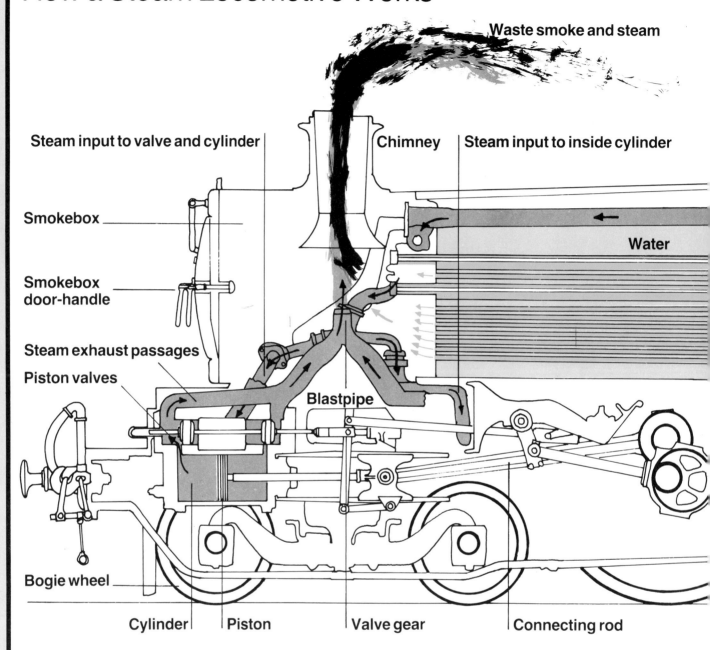

Waste smoke and steam

Steam input to valve and cylinder

Chimney

Steam input to inside cylinder

Smokebox

Water

Smokebox door-handle

Steam exhaust passages

Piston valves

Blastpipe

Bogie wheel

Cylinder

Piston

Valve gear

Connecting rod

This is a cutaway of a Great Western Railway Star Class 4-6-0 locomotive which pulled passenger express trains out of Paddington Station in London to the West of England.

Making a steam engine move can be hard work for the crew. First, a fire has to be lit in the **firebox**. This fire heats up the water in the boiler through a large number of **fire-tubes** along which the heat is drawn.

When it is hot enough, the water begins to turn into **steam**. The driver can decide how much steam he wants to allow to pass through the **steam pipes** to the **cylinders** by working a **regulator handle** in his cab.

In each cylinder there is a **piston** which is pushed backwards and forwards as steam is fed into it, first on one side and then on the other. The exhausted steam comes out of the

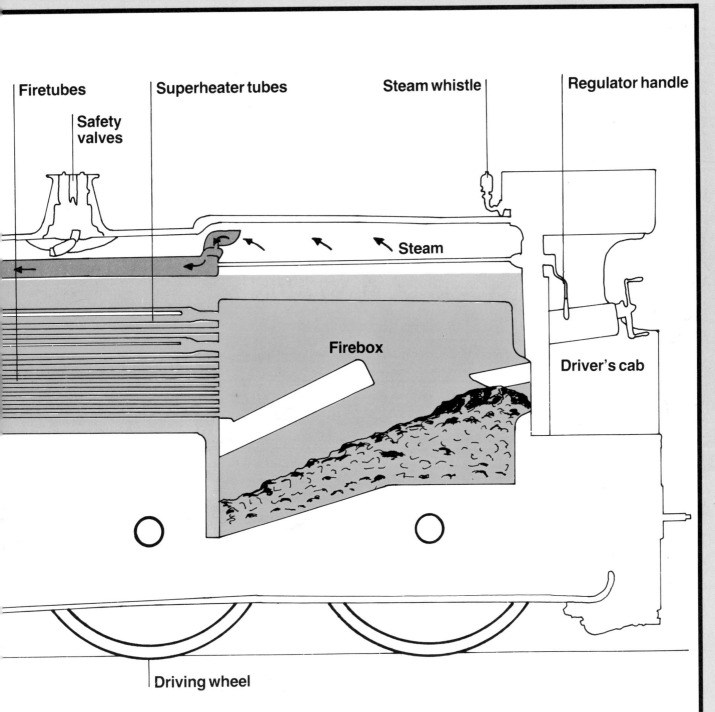

Firetubes

Safety valves

Superheater tubes

Steam whistle

Regulator handle

Steam

Firebox

Driver's cab

Driving wheel

cylinder and is passed up the blastpipe. It is this suction which helps draw the heat down the firetubes towards the front of the engine.

Piston valves control the feeding of the steam into the cylinders. The backward and forward movement of the piston moves a **piston rod**, which is joined to a **connecting rod** and thus to the **driving wheels.**

Waste smoke and steam pass through the **smokebox** and out of the **chimney**, and that is the exhaust smoke that can be seen as the locomotive is driven along. Should steam build up to a dangerous pressure, it can be released through **safety valves** which are located above the boiler.

At the front of the engine are the **bogie wheels**. These are guiding wheels that stabilize the engine.

Famous Locomotives

Some engines earned a world-wide reputation by being huge in size and power. The most famous of the giant steam locomotives were the American *Big Boys* and the slightly smaller British Garratts that operated in South and East Africa from the late 1920s. A Garratt's great boiler was mounted at either end by pivots onto two separate engine units. Monsters like these were often used to haul huge loads of freight over hilly country. They looked magnificent, yet ordinary people were probably more impressed by the sheer speed of certain passenger locomotives.

In Britain and the USA, engines became famous between 1890 and 1939 for their success in winning races against rivals. In Britain such races took place from London northwards into Scotland, and also down to the West Country. For a few years after 1929, a Great Western Railway train, the *Cheltenham Flyer*, claimed that its speeds on its Swindon-London run made it the world's fastest train.

In the USA, on the New York-Chicago route, the New York central line fought its rival with a man who was a born showman running their publicity. George Daniel had sold patent medicines before moving into railway affairs, and in 1893 he made so much of the speed of engine No. 999 pulling the *Empire State Express* that it even appeared on postage stamps.

Around 40 year later, three rival lines between Chicago and St Paul-Minneapolis were the focus of further races. The triumphant *Hiawatha* trains were hauled by 4-4-2 steam locomotives and later by new 4-6-4s capable of matching the diesels run by rivals. Speeds of over 100 miles per hour were no longer remarkable, and the streamlining (the shaping of the locomotives so that they would offer the least resistance to air and so travel faster) was widely practised.

The *Evening Star* was the last of the great steam locomotives built in Britain. This 2-10-0 engine was completed in 1960 and it was the 251st of a very successful type of locomotive.

The *Hardwicke* (left) was a 2-4-0 passenger locomotive of the London and North Western Railway. It won fame in the 1895 races from London to Aberdeen, sharing in achieving the record 8 hour 32 minute run.

The non-stop fast train service which began in 1928 from London to Edinburgh, was called the 'Flying Scotsman'. But *Flying Scotsman* is also the name of the most famous steam locomotive, one of a class which hauled the train in its early years.

This giant engine is called *Big Boy* (above), and 25 of them were built in the USA from 1941 onwards. They were 'articulated' engines with two sets of wheels so that the huge boilers could be carried around sharp curves in the Rockies.

The British high-speed service from Paddington to the west of England rushes across the picturesque river at Bradford-on-Avon. The H.S.T. (High Speed Train) is now a familiar sight on British railway tracks and travels at up to 125 m.p.h.

Building for Railways
Navvies

Tens of thousands of men laboured to build the world's railways. Where lines were built in well-populated areas, the arrival of these navvies was regarded with alarm. In remote areas, navvies had to work in extremes of heat or cold. Navvies building the Union Pacific Line across the USA found the cold so intense at times that drops of spilled coffee froze in a minute and gravy hardened on the plate before it could be eaten.

Picks, shovels and wheelbarrows were all the navvies had to work with. Over the years, railway-building claimed the lives of many of the men in accidents with gunpowder, and falling rocks and earth.

A group of navvies are enjoying a brief rest from their work (left). Although this picture was taken in 1908, railways were still being created by the hard toil of men using picks and shovels. Steam-worked shovels had been available for many years, but it was so easy to find plenty of low-paid workers that few of the railway-building companies actually used machinery. The best tools the men had available to them were wheelbarrows or mulecarts.

Navvies usually lived in cold and uncomfortable huts that could be easily moved. Some of them had their wives with them. They married according to the navvy custom of jumping over a broomstick together.

In well-populated areas navvies fought local people (as well as one another), poached game and were a worry to the police. In 1846 a fight between Irish and English navvies became so fierce that it wrecked the town of Penrith. During the building of the Union Pacific Line, four times as many navvies were murdered in the 'Hell on Wheels' towns whilst celebrating pay day, as ever died in building the line.

Navvies carved a route for the Union Pacific Line across the USA in 1868. This picture (above), taken at the Narrows, Weber Canyon, shows the punishing labour facing the men whenever they had to lay the tracks through a difficult area. Here a path is being smoothed out in stages. A series of shelves is being laid so that rubble can be wheeled away. The Union Pacific used many Irish navvies for the building of their line.

Tunnels

Tunnel-building is one of the most expensive and dangerous activities that face railway builders. Even today, constructing a tunnel is still a slow affair; for early railway-builders it was a plunge into the unknown.

Early tunnels were hacked out by pick, and blasted clear with gunpowder. The navvies worked by flickering candle-light in foul air and – all too often – with water washing over their feet. Tunnels were dug not only from each end, but also from bore-holes drilled along the route. Down these eight- to ten-foot wide holes the men were lowered in buckets to depths of as much as 600 feet. Awaiting the blows of the navvies' picks were unknown dangers like the quicksand area that Robert Stephenson's men struck in the Kilsby Tunnel, where water delayed the work for months.

When it is completed, the Seikan tunnel (above) will, at 33 miles, be the longest in the world. It is being built to link up the main Japanese island of Honshu to the northern island of Hokkaido. The main tunnel is on the right of the picture and the works tunnel is on the left.

It was impossible to avoid tunnel-building in the mountainous land of Switzerland. An electric train (right) clambers up the line that links Chur to the holiday centre of St Moritz. The scene is a reminder of one of the problems that faced the engineers of Swiss railways – great avalanches of snow.

A steam locomotive pulls out of Hawksbury Tunnel in New South Wales, Australia in 1958 (left). In tunnels, fumes, dirt and smoke from the engine easily enter carriages where windows have been left open.

British engineers soon created many tunnels of about two miles in length, and travellers got over their fears that going through them would cause dreadful illnesses. But in other countries there were obstacles far more formidable than those faced in Britain.

The Central Pacific struggled to build eastwards from California through the high Sierras, and 8,000 Chinese navvies toiled to cut a Summit Tunnel amid snowstorms and avalanches. Even more impressive are the tunnels carved through the Alps to link together France, Italy and Switzerland. In Switzerland the Simplon Tunnel is 12 miles long.

Bridges and Viaducts

Across the world, railway engineers faced a common problem – how to carry their track over great rivers, deep ravines, wide estuaries and broad valleys. They solved this problem in all sorts of ways. They created viaducts that were, and are, often beautiful in appearance as well as design. At first they built in iron, brick, stone or timber, and many of these bridges are still in use today. In the twentieth century, however, the most common materials used in building are steel and concrete.

This single-span iron bridge (right) at Sierra Madre Occidentale, is the longest on the Chihuahua Pacific line in Mexico. A modern train can be seen bustling across its 946-foot length.

A train trundles across the elegant Landweis Viaduct (below) on the Rhaetian line in Switzerland. The viaduct was completed in 1914.

In 1890, the Prince of Wales opened a 1½-mile bridge across the Forth near Edinburgh (left). Three giant diamonds, the centre one rooted upon the Inchgarvie rock, stretched out their arms to support one another on the 'cantilever' principle. 1,000-ton weights at either end completed the splendid structure which had taken over 5,000 men seven years to build.

Urban and Suburban Life

At the farm of Monks Coppenhall in the north of England, life went on quietly in the early 19th century. Yet by the 20th century, 42,000 people were crammed onto its former fields. It was the railway that brought about this change. The town created by the Grand Junction line took its name from the nearby home of Lord Crewe. Around the railway workshops the company built houses, a church and a school. It provided a minister, a doctor and two policemen. What happened at Crewe was to be repeated elsewhere.

Workmen leave a train at Victoria Station, London, in 1868 (below). Many railway companies did not try to welcome working people as their customers. In the 1840s the British government compelled companies to take ordinary people in third-class carriages for one penny a mile. The carriages had to have seats and be properly roofed. Some railway companies replied by running such 'parliamentary' trains at very awkward times.

People coming into London pour off trains at Liverpool Street Station in 1928 (below). By 1854, about 10,000 people were coming regularly into London by train.

Many people could not afford the fares and walked, took horse buses and (later) trams. But the Great Eastern offered a ten-mile return trip for twopence, an example other companies followed in the 20th century. The age of the commuter had arrived.

UNDERGROUND

SANCTUARY.

"Tis pleasant, through the loopholes of retreat,
To peep at such a world; to see the stir
Of the great Babel, and not feel the crowd;
To hear the roar she sends through all her gates
At a safe distance, where the dying sound
Falls a soft murmur on th' uninjured ear."
William Cowper

Many people were able to live well away from their place of work as a result of railway-building (left). In 1907, the Hampstead tube in London joined Charing Cross to what was then open country at Golders Green. Inside five years, many houses had been built near the station and builders were urging people to move out of the city.

Today, throughout the world, commuters pour into cities. These Japanese travellers (above) are leaving their train in Tokyo. When they return they will find special 'people packers' waiting to push as many of them as possible into the carriages of the train.

Towns were transformed by trains. The railways contributed to the smoky grime that industry smeared over buildings, they gobbled up land for track and they created great constructions that loomed over houses. Yet the trains also brought townspeople a speedy postal service, stories from all over the world in national newspapers and fresh food. The Scottish poet, William McGonagall, thought that Dundee housewives' shopping would be helped by trains:

> 'By bringing cheap tea, bread and jam
> And also some of Lipton's ham.'

Coast and Country Life

One Saturday in 1842, dozens of Sunday-school teachers in the cotton town of Preston were busy trying to control well over 2,000 excited children. The whole party was about to set off for a day's holiday to Fleetwood. A recently-built railway line had made the outing possible.

Before the coming of railways, holidays away from home were only possible for the wealthy, but in the 1840s there was a spurt of track-building to the coast. Little villages exploded in size. Blackpool grew from a few hundred folk to 47,000 in 1907. Hotels and boarding-houses were built and some coastal places, like Southampton, grew into ports from which passengers could sail across the English Channel.

Britain's countryside was opened up by many branch lines (right). To farmers the railway was very important. Fresh milk, vegetables, fruit and eggs could easily be sent into cities, and animals could be packed into trucks instead of having to be driven many miles to market. Country folk could now buy cheaper coal, goods made by industries and other materials.

Southend was a fashionable seaside resort before the railway age (below), but the railway meant that its attractions could be offered to thousands of working people.

UNDERGROUND

Ruislip Village
and all around lie the
quiet fields and lanes.

BOOK TO
RUISLIP.

Cheap Return Tickets
on Sundays.

Famous Stations

Early railways did not need stations. They were built to carry goods, not people. Passengers who travelled on the early lines used inns along the way. The Liverpool-Manchester line changed all that by providing special buildings for travellers, including one at Manchester which was complete with booking-hall and waiting-rooms.

Once the early railway companies had recovered from their surprise at the popularity of their passenger trains, they began to provide stations in all sorts of designs and materials. In villages and towns, the station was one of the most important buildings in the community. In it was a telegraph office and often (in the late 19th century) a bookstall. Railway companies also built very grand stations to show how safe, reliable and important their services were, and tried to provide every facility.

Jacoma Station, Washington (above) is unusual in its design, and looks almost like an opera-house.

The station where many passengers coming to Paris on long-distance trains alight is the Gare de Lyons (right).

Its imposing structure makes Frankfurt Station in Germany memorable (left).

One of the biggest of the Victorian buildings in London is St Pancras Station (below). It was designed by Giles Gilbert Scott and W. H. Barlow for the Midland Railway and opened to business in 1869. London stations had changed greatly since the first steam-line terminus at London Bridge. Passengers here had climbed stairs to open platforms on a viaduct. An old sail was hung up to shelter them in stormy weather.

Moving Goods and People

In 1840, a British jury decided that a man had died 'from cold and exposure while travelling in a second-class carriage of the Great Western Railways'.

Early travellers had to be tough. First-class passengers sat in carriages that looked like several stage-coach bodies joined together. Early third-class passengers journeyed in open waggons which were often called 'Stanhopes' ('stand ups'), so poorly were they provided with comfort. The Manchester-Liverpool line kindly drilled holes in the waggon floors so that the water could drain away.

These people (right) from Europe have landed at Locust Point, Baltimore, USA in 1880. Railroads of the time encouraged immigration from Europe. The fares they charged these people and the land they sold brought the companies a great deal of money.

The Santa Fe Company persuaded 15,000 Germans living in Russia to leave and settle in Kansas. They proved to be such good farmers that other companies tried to kidnap groups of them! The immigrants often found that the land they had bought was not very good.

George Pullman designed this 'Pioneer' coach (above) in 1865. For people who were able to afford the price, coaches like this made long journeys across the USA far more comfortable. They provided proper places in which the passengers could sleep. Pullman improved his coaches and sold so many that he became a millionaire.

These passengers of the 1870s (left) are settling down for the night in a carriage of the Union Pacific Railway. Early carriages had candles but, by this time, kerosene lamps were being used.

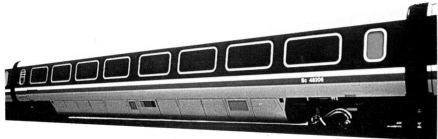

This is one of the coaches that will be used on British Rail's Advanced Passenger Train (left). The shape of the carriage narrows from its waist up since the train tilts as it speeds around curves in the track.

The coach is very like other modern British coaches, being made of steel and fitted with wide doors, double-glazed windows and air-conditioning. British Rail has steadily abandoned coaches that have lots of separate compartments in them.

Long journeys were so common in the USA that much longer coaches were developed. Instead of separate compartments, the American coaches were open, with gangways down the middle. Passenger traffic increased so much from 1870 to 1900 that in Europe and the USA, improved coaches were produced. They ran on bogies, instead of fixed wheels, and had better lighting, lavatories and corridors.

The Orient Express

On 5th June 1883, a worried Georges Nagelmackers stood by the brand new train he had bought for a fortune. It was waiting to carry passengers from Paris to Constantinople. In fact, wealthy people flocked in large numbers to travel on the train, attracted by the adventurous journey and by the luxury of the carriages. Turkish carpets and silk-lined walls surrounded the customers in their drawing-rooms on the *Orient Express*. There were showers, and a very lavish dining-room which served first-class food. One of the keenest customers was King Boris of Bulgaria.

This poster (above), advertising the *Orient Express*, shows some of the wealthy passengers who used it. A ticket for a servant cost as much as his wages for a whole year!

Mystery and adventure have always been linked with this train. Several writers have used it in their stories. Here (right), the film *Murder on the Orient Express* is being shot.

Great Express Trains

Before air-travel began to draw away customers, most countries had great express train services. These trains were often painted in special colours and fitted with extra comforts. Many of them ran right across countries, and some even crossed whole continents. They attracted well-to-do businessmen and holiday-makers, and they helped to unite countries by linking remote areas.

These expresses even brought about the growth of new places. In France, the *Blue Train*, running from Calais down to the Mediterranean coast, did much to cause the expansion of holiday centres like Nice. In each of its expensively decorated coaches there used to be an attendant to care for the travellers. The great hotels of the south of France owe much to this express train.

One of the oldest expresses in the USA, the *North Coast Limited*, linked Chicago and Seattle. At Homestake Pass the line reached a height of 1,928 metres and the train had nurses on board to give oxygen to passengers.

A locomotive on the Canadian Pacific line hauls coaches through the Rocky Mountains (above). The line climbs steep slopes and passes through forest and swamp land.

A *Super Chief* express on the Santa Fe line speeds through Arizona, watched by Navajo Indians busy at their weaving.

The Rheingold Express (right) carries passengers in great comfort from the Hook of Holland right through Germany to Switzerland.

An express on Australia's Transcontinental Line travels across the Nullabor Plain (below right). This is the longest stretch of straight track in the world – 297 miles.

Passengers Around the World

In 1854, an American visitor to Britain wrote, 'I am not a timid man but I never enter an English railway carriage without having in my pocket a loaded revolver. How am I to know but that my travelling companion may be a madman or a criminal?' Travellers on British trains who got into difficulties were, until the late 19th century, without reliable means of calling for help. One railway guide advised travellers that when trains entered tunnels, 'It is always well to have the hands and arms ready for defence.'

As long-distance passenger services developed, travellers faced the problems caused by the absence of lavatories in carriages. Desperate passengers rushed from the cars whenever the train stopped at a station. One Victorian lady remembered journeys for which her nanny made for the children 'newspaper potties which were later thrown from the window'.

Travellers on early trains crossing the USA passed the time in their open cars singing and playing cards, as well as peering at the scenery. Some early Pullmans had organs installed to help the singing. On Sundays, a service was usually held in one of the cars.

The orderly passengers on the Alaska Railroad (above) are in complete contrast to those on the Indian trains (above left).

The cold weather in Alaska means that the heating in the carriages is vital.

In India, travellers cram into the coaches, perch on top of the carriages and hang off the sides. The Indian train services provide cheap travel to many towns and villages that would otherwise be cut off, and this is very important to people, few of whom can afford cars.

These passengers, colourfully dressed in hand-printed clothes, are boarding a train in Volta, West Africa (right). The continent of Africa has been, and is being opened up by the introduction of railroads. Africa is divided into many different countries and the transport of goods and medicines is a problem. The railway systems have made it possible to transport goods, and they have also improved the lines of communication between different communities.

Marshalling-Yards

Railways developed partly because they were so useful for moving heavy loads. Special areas called 'marshalling-yards' were built where different waggon-loads were sorted out and grouped to make up trains for different destinations.

Yards like these are often to be found at ports and in big cities. A modern marshalling-yard is divided into two sections. Locomotives bring in the waggons to a 'receiving' yard. From there they are shunted into a big 'classifications' yard where they are grouped into trains. A shunting-engine pushes waggons over a hump and they then run downhill into different sidings.

A man operating a computer is in charge of the work. The computer gathers information about each waggon and then controls the sorting-out by working the points and braking the waggons when necessary.

The Alyth marshalling-yard in Calgary, Canada (above) is a place where waggons full of the produce from the great wheat-growing areas mix with trucks carrying minerals.

All sorts of different freight waggons can be seen (right) in the Mainz marshalling-yard in Germany. They are waiting for the locomotives which will pull them to arrive.

Railways in Wartime

On 2nd December 1854, hundreds of navvies tried to crowd into an office in London. They were eager to take their railway-building skills out to the Crimea where British troops were fighting the Russians. They did travel out there and, in the Crimea, they helped to alter the progress of the war. They speedily built a supply-line from the port up to army positions. Where once there had only been a bad road, now supplies could be moved easily on a new road.

Before long, the generals of many countries were having to think hard about how best to use this new development. German generals, in particular, were interested in the use of railways. In a war against France in 1870, they were helped to victory by the speedy way in which they could gather huge forces on France's frontiers.

These soldiers (below) are waiting to board a train which will take them to one of the terrible battle-fronts of the 1st World War (1914-1918). All the countries that fought in this war used railways to collect and move their armies, and German generals even played a big part in planning the building of Germany's lines.

Close to the battle-fronts, light railways were built that were used to move up men and supplies and bring back the wounded. Britain alone sent 184,475 railway men to the war; over 21,000 of them died there. There were countless railwaymen like Herbert Evans, who took his little engine up and down the two-foot gauge track to the Ypres trenches.

From 1904 to 1905 war raged between Japan and Russia. Many battles were fought in northern China. The Russians were badly beaten, yet it was the building of a railway that had helped them think that they could win. The Trans-Siberian Line seemed to offer the chance to move large armies east to the battle-front. These Japanese soldiers (above) are busy wrecking part of the track.

During the terrible American Civil War, when the North and South fought one another, railways played an important part in moving men and supplies. They also provided adventure stories like the one about the capture, in 1862, of a locomotive called the *General* by a party of desperate men from the North who had raided deep into Southern territory. For nearly 90 miles, they steamed at top speed back to their own lines, chased by Southern soldiers on another engine, the *Texas*. When the *General* ran out of fuel, the raiders were caught.

In China, railways helped to cause a war in 1900. China was very weak and other countries were trying to make money by controlling parts of that vast land. Railway-building was part of this spread of foreign control.

This railway line is being bombed during the Second World War (1939-1945). By this time, the development of road transport meant that railways were not quite so essential in wartime. However, their great importance is shown by the way each side tried hard to weaken the other by destroying railways with air attacks.

Most bombing raids were not very accurate, and big targets like marshalling-yards were attractive because they were easy to hit, and they were also important places where supplies could be destroyed.

Off the Rails

According to an early Victorian magazine, a man leaving his family for a rail journey ought to tell them,

> 'I'm going by the Rail, my dears, where the engines
> puff and hiss;
> And ten to one the chances are that something
> goes amiss.'

Accidents were alarmingly common when railways were first developed. Locomotive boilers blew up, especially when a foolish driver had tied down the safety valves. Faulty track led to trains coming off the rails – this was very common in the USA. American travellers also ran the risk of accidents which were caused by trains ploughing into herds of cattle. After one such accident in Nevada, the passengers calmly butchered the cattle and cooked steaks while they were waiting to be rescued.

A disaster in Armagh, Ireland, in 1889 (above). There were no automatic brakes at that time and the coaches ran away down a hill. It was this accident that led to the compulsory fitting of automatic brakes.

Divers are searching the waters of the River Tay, Scotland (left), for the wreckage of an engine, five carriages and a brake-van. The train plunged off as the bridge collapsed during a fearful storm on 28th December 1879. The disaster was blamed on Sir Thomas Bouch, the designer, and on faulty construction work. 78 people lost their lives.

In 1842, a French disaster claimed 53 lives. The locomotive's main axle snapped, the coaches crashed into the engine and fire broke out. The passengers had been locked into their compartments.

Railway companies helped cause accidents in the 19th century by making drivers and signalmen work for too many hours a day. Railway staff hurt in accidents found it hard to get compensation. The companies tried to claim that accidents were 'Acts of God'.

Some disasters were caused on purpose. In the USA, several gangs of bandits, the most famous led by Jesse James, roamed the more remote stretches of track. They levered rails out of place to cause a crash. Then they rushed among the shaken passengers and robbed them. They were often able to gallop away before help could arrive.

Unusual Railways
Narrow Gauge

By the end of the 19th century many important railway lines had been built. Plans for new lines sometimes worried the men setting them up, for the routes where most money was to be made were often already finished. A cheaper sort of line was developed in which the track gauge was much narrower than usual. This sort of line could go round quite sharp corners and clamber up hillsides without expensive earthworks and tunnels having to be built. Lines like this were also popular in places like mines and quarries where just a short stretch of track was needed.

Narrow-gauge lines in Britain were not common and, until 1863, those that did exist were worked by horses. Then the North Festiniog line began to use small steam locomotives to pull waggons filled with slate from Festiniog quarries. In 1865 this line began to take passengers too. It was so successful that other Welsh companies copied it and so did people in other countries. Visitors even arrived from as far away as Russia to inspect the little trains trundling along the tiny track.

Not only the mine and quarry owners, but also farmers growing crops like sugar that needed moving to factories, were ready to adopt the narrow gauge. In countries like Switzerland and Ireland, cheap lines on a small gauge were laid, and they ran to small and remote villages that had been ignored by the main-line railways.

A train on the Welshpool and Llanfair Railway line (above). This 2½-foot gauge line first opened in 1903. It closed in 1956, but volunteers have worked on it and part of it opened up again in 1963. On it can be seen a remarkable range of locomotives and rolling-stock from the West Indies, West Africa and Austria.

A train to Darjeeling (left). The line through the Himalayan mountains to Darjeeling was built as cheaply as possible. There are no tunnels and few bridges. Instead the track zig-zags and spirals upwards on very steep gradients. The 55-mile journey takes seven hours.

The Denver and Rio Grande Line in Colorado, USA (right) was built up into the mountains in the 1870s and 1880s. The track is three feet wide. Part of it is still used to carry tourists through magnificent forest and mountain scenery.

Mountain Railways

At first, trains clambered up short, steep sections of track hauled by ropes attached to stationary steam engines. For a time they even left Euston Station in London in this way. The problem of long climbs up steep gradients was solved by the adoption of ideas like John Blenkinsop's scheme for a cogwheel which slotted into teeth on a track. *Novelty*'s designer, Eriksson, suggested a system of spring wheels gripping a centre rail.

The building of railways in mountainous Switzerland from 1847 caused great tunnels to be bored, like the St Gotthard Tunnel in 1882. Where the climb was very steep, Swiss engineers built various forms of racked railway with a toothed wheel on the locomotive which slotted into a central ladder-like track. Many engineers have used this method to carry tourists to the tops of mountains.

For 77 years, the line from Wellington to Napier, New Zealand, included a 2½-mile stretch with a very steep gradient. British-built steam locomotives – sometimes five to a train – struggled slowly up the slope of this Rimutuka incline (left). It is by-passed now, but while it operated it was the world's best example of the system by which powerfully-sprung horizontal wheels gripped a centre rail. This system was first designed by James Fell.

This electric locomotive is pulling a train on the Swiss Berne-Lotschberg-Simplon line (below). The line was electrified from its opening in 1913, and is linked to the Simplon Tunnel.

A train climbs up Mount Washington, New Hampshire, USA (above). Sylvester Marsh created this route in 1869, realizing that tourists would flock to travel on a spectacular train ride to a mountain peak.

The Schafbergbahn-Dampfbetrieb line is one of the two steam-operated railways in Austria that use the popular 'rack' system for climbing steep gradients. The racked track, with a points change, can be clearly seen here (right).

Underground Railways

By the mid-19th century many of the world's cities had streets crowded with horse-drawn vehicles. Several engineers, therefore, began to work on building underground railways. On 10th January 1863, the world's first underground railway opened for business. The Metropolitan line was built close to the surface by digging a deep trench through the street and supporting the sides with walls and the roof with brick arches or iron girders.

The Metropolitan line prospered and expanded and, in 1890, the world's first electric tube line, the City and Southern, opened. This line – also in London – lay too deeply underground to be built by trenching. Instead, its engineer, James Greathead, bored a tunnel using a shield inside which workmen cut away the soil. London's blue clay proved ideal for tunnelling.

Across the world, other cities began to follow London's example. The next European city to adopt the underground was Budapest. Here, a 2½-mile line opened in 1896.

Passengers use the Paris Metro (above). The Metro first opened in 1900 and was developed rapidly in the 1920s. Since 1950, it has experimented with the use of smooth-running rolling-stock with rubber tyres. The trains travel on concrete surfaces which are laid outside the normal track in the tunnels.

To cities crowded with traffic, undergrounds continue to be attractive. They provide speedy travel without the destruction of historic buildings on the surface.

When lines were built deep beneath the surface, the problem of reaching the station from the street had to be solved. The answer appeared at Earls Court in London, in 1911, in the shape of a moving staircase or 'escalator'. Passengers of the time were at first so fearful of using this novelty that the railway company paid a man with a wooden leg to ride up and down to prove its safety. Today, many new undergrounds are being built or planned.

This photograph (above) shows a section of the Madrid underground being built in the 1920s. This system first opened in 1919. It was built on the 'cut and fill' system often used for lines near street-surface level. 'Cut and fill' meant that deep trenches were dug in the streets, the line was laid, and then the street surface was smoothed over again.

This picture was taken (right) when work was in progress on the construction of the newest of London's underground lines – the Jubilee line. The first part of the line, from Charing Cross to Baker Street, opened in May 1979. The deep level of the line meant that it had to be built by the much more expensive tunnel-boring system.

Eccentric Railways

When engineers first experimented with railways, all sorts of unusual ideas appeared. In 1815, visitors to Butterly Iron Works, near Derby, might have seen a strange iron monster hissing steam and 'walking' slowly and carefully along the railway line.

This 'engine that walked' was the idea of William Brunton. Steam power drove two huge legs fitted with feet and ankle-joints at a steady 2½ miles per hour. Unfortunately the creature was unable to go backwards. During one of its tests the machine exploded, killing not only the crew but also several people who had come up to peer closely at it.

This carriage (above) was moved along by the pressure of air. Designed by Christopher Nickels in 1845, it was one of the first 'atmospheric' railways.

A train glides along the top of a concrete beam in Disneyland, California (right). It gives passengers a smooth ride and splendid views.

Several engineers tried to design railways worked by the atmosphere. The first plan was to put trains inside huge canvas tubes, suck air from the front of the tube with pumps and let air pressure from behind move the train along. This was so unworkable that it was soon dropped in favour of having a small tube running between the tracks.

Brunel himself designed one of these railways, the South Devon line. The top of the tube had a slot in it to allow the piston in the tube to be joined to the train. The line worked only briefly in 1847.

An Irish train is carefully balanced across a single rail (left). From 1887 to 1924, this little train steamed up and down between the market town of Listowel and the seaside resort of Ballybunion. The train had to be loaded very carefully. If too many passengers or livestock were piled into one side of the train, it was likely to tip up.

The Wuppertal-Sonnborn monorail train in West Germany hangs below its trackway (right). This service has operated since 1901.

Railway People

Railways provided jobs for many people. Largely for safety reasons, railway workers' lives were full of rules and regulations, which were stricter than transport workers had ever met before. Many companies used soldiers to take charge of their hundreds of workers. Train crews were not allowed to drink alcohol and one railwayman was even sacked for betting on a horse race.

With the introduction of railways came the introduction of a standard 'railway time', and stationmasters had to carry watches in order to keep to the timetable. Today, the regulations and strict time-keeping seem quite normal.

The driver of a train on French Railways sits in a warm and comfortable cab (below). He has to concentrate on his skilful work, but it is far less tiring than that done by steam locomotive drivers. The men who drove the steam trains sometimes seemed like heroes to their passengers. An American driver, Harry Easton, once took his train-load of passengers safely over a causeway swept by floods which had been whipped up by a hurricane. He had to crash aside a wrecked house. Although less dangerous now, the driver's job is a very responsible one.

This chef (above) is preparing a meal to be served in a French Railways dining-car. Early travellers had to grab food at short stops in stations. From the 1870s onwards, dining-cars began to appear in Britain and the USA and some companies sold baskets of food.

Today, many trains have at least a buffet car, while the long-distance train usually has a dining-car with a choice of menu. It is easier to cook on board train now because of the smoother running.

The station-master at Calais Maritime in the north of France waits to see off a steam-hauled train (left). Climbing into the cab is the fireman. His job of shovelling fuel into a firebox on a draughty, swaying footplate was one of the hardest on the railways. Locomotives like this *Pacific* easily ate up six tons of coal on a trip.

By this Indian Railways locomotive at Amortsar (below) is standing a man whose job it is to provide the travellers with tea. He is called the 'char wallah'.

Signalling

As railways grew from short, single lines into bigger systems, the railway companies had to find ways of stopping their trains from crashing into one another. At first most companies used railway policemen who stood by the track and signalled with their arms or with flags to show drivers if the way ahead was safe. At points where tracks divided, the lonely pointsman waited to work a switch when he heard the shriek of the whistle of an approaching train.

As train speeds increased, drivers could not see the policemen in time. All sorts of boards and discs were invented, and fixed on tall poles and moved about to show danger or safety. American companies used tall masts up which a ball was hoisted to show that there was clear track up ahead. Semaphore signals gradually became the most popular form of warning. The signal arm was moved up and down by wires worked from nearby signal-boxes.

The coming of the electric telegraph meant that messages could be passed between signal-boxes to show whether the stretch of line controlled by each man was safe to enter. In icy weather, the signal wires froze and men had to be paid to keep fires burning and the signals working freely.

Today, modern equipment and the use of computers mean that signalling is much safer and more efficient.

Colour signals (above) have largely replaced the older types. These are in Essen.

The old style of semaphore signal is shown here (right) at Carnforth in the north of England. The signals are in the 'stop' position.

Today's signal controller sits in front of boxes, buttons and switches, like this operator in Munich, Germany (left). He uses power-operated signals and is in charge of many miles of track.

ON THE TRACK

Track is being re-laid on the Baltimore and Ohio line, USA. Early railway track was made in short lengths, but as iron and steel working improved, longer lengths could be made.

The track was usually fastened onto wooden sleepers. In Britain, Joseph Locke developed a rail that slotted into a 'chair'. Charles Vignoles produced a flat-bottomed rail that could be spiked onto the sleepers. Here, some rails are being laid onto a concrete bed.

Railway track has to be constantly checked and repaired if accidents are to be avoided. Great armies of men were once needed for this.

Today, the work can be carried out with the help of machines. This curious-looking machine is automatic and is used for lifting track and levelling the ballast which the rails lie on. It is at work on the Baltimore line in the USA. The use of modern equipment means that repairs of this kind can be carried out rapidly.

In the Station

As railways grew, companies gathered together people who could work in and around the stations, as well as on the trains. There were jobs that involved loading and unloading, helping passengers with luggage, selling tickets, cleaning and checking the trains and working in offices. Men came in large numbers to work for the railways because they provided a career in which a man who did well in one job could be promoted to a better one.

The companies made all sorts of rules. In 1842, the Great Western Railway expected porters to be at least 5 feet 9 inches tall, and able to read and write. The Taff Vale company went further than most by insisting that its men went to church. In 1855, it said, 'Rule 26, Every person on Sundays when he is not on duty will attend a place of worship as it will be the means of promotion.'

In charge of all these people was the station-master. He usually wore a special uniform which was quite distinctive.

Railway staff wait on the station at Mainz, in Germany for the 12.43 train to pull away from the platform (left). On the left of the picture is the reservations clerk who is directing a passenger to her seat.

Today, in Europe and America, indicator panels usually provide passengers with information.

In Europe and the USA, the railways still operate according to a very complicated rule-book. The countries of the Far East, however, do not necessarily have such rigid systems. Whereas most stations in the western world now have motorized trolleys which are used for transporting passengers' luggage, the stations in India and Africa generally have poorly-paid porters who have to carry luggage by hand or on their heads.

A group of porters waits on the station platform at Ahmedabad in India. The Indian Railways are owned and run by the Indian government. They provide more jobs for Indians than any other employer in the country. Today, around one and a half million people work for the Indian Railways, either in or around the station.

Today and Tomorrow
Diesel and Electric Locomotives

Though powerful and splendid to see, steam locomotives spread dirt, were hard work to operate and took a while to get up steam. When motorcars began to be built, in the late 19th century, several inventors developed trains that were really buses on rails. In 1903, Britain's North Eastern Railway ran an experimental coach and, 15 years later, a Ford bus with its wheels changed to fit track. By 1914, many such vehicles were being used in the USA, but petrol was expensive and it easily exploded in accidents.

In 1898, Dr Rudolf Diesel, a German inventor, showed the world the diesel engine he had been improving since he had invented it five years earlier. The initial cost of running diesel engines was much higher, but they saved on manpower and they were more economic because they could be in service almost continually. Soon many diesel-powered trains were working on short lines. Dr Diesel tried to promote his engine, visiting the USA to do so, until 1913 when he mysteriously disappeared overboard from a ferry.

The electric locomotive (above) is being tested in a workshop for the French National Railways – the S.N.C.F. It is one of the very powerful express engines built to pull heavy trains at high speeds. This locomotive, like many S.N.C.F. long-distance engines, is able to draw on the power of more than one voltage system.

This (below) is a diagram of the diesel-electric locomotive, known as the Class 47, which is used by British Rail to haul passenger trains.

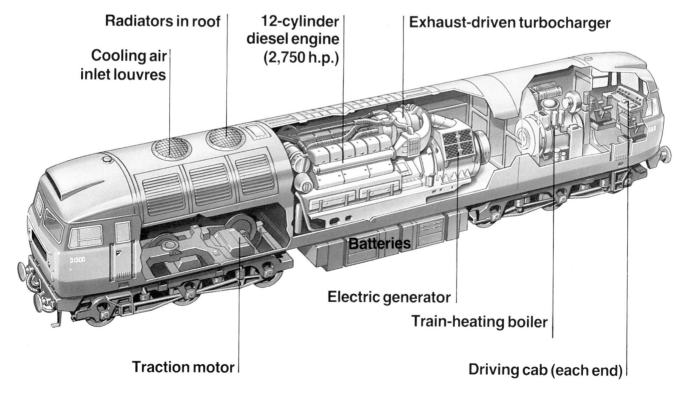

Radiators in roof

Cooling air inlet louvres

12-cylinder diesel engine (2,750 h.p.)

Exhaust-driven turbocharger

Batteries

Electric generator

Train-heating boiler

Traction motor

Driving cab (each end)

The power of electricity was well known at the time George Stephenson was building the Manchester-Liverpool line, but it was some years before it was harnessed to drive trains. In the USA, Thomas Davenport of Vermont demonstrated an electric engine as early as 1837. At an exhibition in Berlin in 1879, Werner von Siemens operated a successful electric locomotive and went on, in 1881, to help found the world's first electric line which provided regular passenger services at Lichterfields.

Electric trains became most popular in countries short of coal, like Switzerland. Today, they are being installed in many countries because they can use power generated by coal, oil, hydro or nuclear power.

Diesel engines, like this S.N.C.F. locomotive, were cheaper to operate in the long term than the steam engines that they replaced. A diesel engine was operating in a dockyard as early as 1894.

Trains for Fun

The gradual disappearance of steam locomotives from the tracks of many countries has not reduced interest in these machines. In Europe and in North America especially, enthusiastic people have kept steam trains running. Railway engines and their rolling-stock have been rescued and lovingly restored; railway track and stations have been carefully maintained.

All this has had to be done in spare time with money that is often difficult to scrape together. But when the work is over and the steam-line re-opens – usually along only a few miles – people flock to travel on these preserved trains, to photograph the fine sight of steam locomotives at work and to record their sounds.

Not all of these railways, so popular with holiday-makers, are full-size. There are many narrow-gauge lines which were once built for practical work and now carry thousands of tourists on sight-seeing trips.

Britain is a small enough country to be able to draw people to these railways quite easily. Many of the lines are in beautiful parts of the country to which tourists go anyway. But in the vast area of the USA some restored lines have failed. Successful ones sometimes try and please customers by offering them all sorts of extra entertainments like mock raids by bandits and Indians, like the Tweetsie Railroad in North Carolina. Others flourish because they offer tourists a chance to re-live part of America's history.

The Strasburg Railway, for example, takes passengers through parts of Pennsylvania which are famous for being settled by people from Europe in the 17th and 18th centuries. In the USA and in Britain, there are plenty of people who are eager to ride in steam trains over track normally worked by diesel or electric locomotives.

The last train of the day steams cheerfully along the Bluebell line in Sussex. The route is one of many which have been restored by keen enthusiasts. The Bluebell line was taken over after British Rail abandoned it as a branch line.

A scene on the 15-inch gauge Romney, Hythe and Dymchurch line in Kent (above). The line opened in 1927-29 and is worked by miniature steam locomotives based on eight L.N.E.R. or Canadian Pacific types.

Passengers are waiting to board the Tallylyn Railway's narrow-gauge train (above left). This line was first built to move slate from a quarry.

This steam locomotive (left) is pulling coach-loads of tourists along the three miles of one of the USA's most entertaining lines – the Tweetsie Railroad in North Carolina. During their ride, the passengers are treated to mock attacks, first by bandits and then by Indians.

Passengers travelling on the
Fairborne Railway near
Barmouth in North Wales
(above). This is one of the
many midget railways that can
be found in parks, gardens,
zoos and seaside resorts.
These tiny engines can be
powerful enough to pull quite
long trains of eager customers.
They provide entertainment for
customers and a hobby for
railway enthusiasts.

This picture (left) shows part of
the great Indian Rail Transport
Museum that is being built up in
New Delhi.

   Preserving engines and
rolling-stock in this way has
interested people for nearly a
century. Fine museums can
be visited at York, Lucerne,
Baltimore, Mulhouse and
many other places.

Modern High-Speed Railways

On 1st October 1967, great crowds of excited people gathered in Tokyo Station. Alongside the platform lay the object they had come to see – a gleaming stream-lined train. These spectators were looking at the *Bullet* train (or Tokaido express), one of the world's greatest expresses.

Before those fortunate enough to travel on the train lay a 320-mile journey to Osaka over brand new track, specially laid out with gentle curves so that speeds up to 130 miles per hour could be safely reached. Though costly to create, the line was carefully built through the most crowded part of Japan. The line has proved to be enormously popular and, on one day in 1969, carried a total of 520,000 passengers.

This success encouraged railway companies in other countries to develop their own fast trains. In Britain, former aircraft designers produced plans for the A.P.T. (Advanced Passenger Train). This invention was intended to run at high speeds over existing track by means of wheel systems that steered themselves round the curves and carriages that tilted inwards when necessary.

The A.P.T. has been dogged by difficulties, but the 125-miles per hour H.S.T. (Higher Speed Train) produced by traditional railway engineers, has been more successful. Since its first run on the London-Bristol route in 1977, the H.S.T. has become a common sight on British railways.

France, too, has created a high-speed train. The T.G.V. (*Train Grande Vitesse*) travels the 265 miles from Paris to Lyons on new track in two hours, before continuing on its way on the general railway system. Like the British, they run their high-speed trains on lines used by slower traffic.

Such triumphs have provided the railways in many countries with a powerful reply to the challenge of other forms of transport which threatened their existence.

The stream-lined shape of the Japanese Bullet Train streaks past Mount Fujiyama. Snow sheds and snow-melting sprinklers are being provided on mountainous stretches.

Index